KEY WEST

Dan O'Brien

I0139562

BROADWAY PLAY PUBLISHING INC
New York
www.broadwayplaypublishing.com
info@broadwayplaypublishing.com

Cover photo by Bill Jackson

First edition: November 2020
I S B N: 978-0-88145-873-2

Book design: Marie Donovan
Page make-up: Adobe InDesign
Typeface: Palatino

for Jessica

KEY WEST was originally commissioned by Manhattan Theatre Club, with subsequent development at theaters including Williamstown Theatre Festival, Magic Theatre, and Rattlestick Playwrights Theater.

KEY WEST received a lab presentation with The Play Company (Artistic Directors, Kate Loewald & Jack Temchin) at the McGinn Cazale Theatre in New York City on 18-22 September 2001. The cast and creative contributor were:

NIALL...Michael Cullen
BRIGID.. Aidan Sullivan

Director.. Daniel Gerroll

KEY WEST premiered at Geva Theatre Center (Artistic Director, Mark Cuddy; Managing Director, John Quinlivan; Executive Director, Nan Hildebrandt) in Rochester, New York on 3 November 2004. The cast and creative contributors were:

NIALL...Richard Elmore
BRIGID...Lori Prince

Director...Skip Greer
Scenic design...Rob Koharchik
Costume design...Maria Marrero
Lighting design... Kendall Smith
Sound design.. William Pickens
Assistant director................................... Kimberly Arnold
Dramaturg... Marge Betley
Stage manager...Emily M Arnold
Apprentice stage manager ....Alexandra Backus
Production manager .... Joel Markus
Casting........................Elissa Myers, Paul Fouquet, C S A

CHARACTERS & SETTING

Brigid, *early 20s*
Niall, *early 50s*

Time: September
Place: Key West

One: Niall's *bar, night*
Two: The beach, two nights later
Three: Niall's *studio, the same night*

NOTES

(1) Dialogue in quotes and parentheses, i.e. ("Yes.") or ("No."), indicates a nonverbal response.

(2) Isolated ellipses in the dialogue

...

or

...?

indicate significant beats, often played as pauses.

(3) The play runs about 90 minutes without an intermission.

"A ghost is someone."
Robert Lowell

One:
"North"

BRIGID: Sorry to bother you, but I seem to have lost my keys.

(BRIGID's *at the door, wet from the rain; storm outside.*)

(NIALL's *playing a game with cards.*)

BRIGID: Excuse me:

NIALL: What are the chances?

BRIGID: I beg your pardon?

NIALL: Coming to Key West and two straight days of rain…

BRIGID: —Three actually.

NIALL: —Has it been three already?

BRIGID: It's the third day.

NIALL: Gets so you lose count around here. I live here, I have to live here, but a person like you— (*He turns and looks her up and down.*) …

BRIGID: …Yes… Well, you see, my keys—

NIALL: (*His cards*) —We're closed, by the way.

BRIGID: The sign says open.

NIALL: Does it?

BRIGID: Yes.

NIALL: Flip it around—

BRIGID: It's not even eleven o'clock—

NIALL: It's half eleven, the weather's Biblical—flip the God damned—!

(BRIGID *does.*)

NIALL: Thank you. Now:

BRIGID: —You're welcome.

NIALL: What's wrong with you?

BRIGID: I told you: I have lost the keys to my car and—

NIALL: Did you now?

BRIGID: —Yes. —And I have reason to believe they might be here.

NIALL: Did you know that the human body is nearly eighty percent water?

BRIGID: …I think I've read that somewhere…

NIALL: Doesn't make much sense, now does it? I mean, that *can not* be true: if you tried to touch someone they'd just slip right through your fingers…

BRIGID: …

NIALL: Where'd you lose them?

BRIGID: Who?

NIALL: Your keys, my girl—

BRIGID: *(Not shouting)* —If I knew that I wouldn't be here now would I?

NIALL: —There's no reason to shout, my dear…

BRIGID: Sorry… Sorry.

NIALL: *(Getting up)* No, I'm sorry—*I'm* the one who should be sorry:
Please, do, sit:

(BRIGID *does.*)

NIALL: Close your eyes.

BRIGID: —Why?

NIALL: —Close them! There: now I want you to think:

BRIGID: ...About?

NIALL: —Backwards: think back in time. We're going
to find your lost keys... You can remember anything if
you just think long enough for it...
...Now: where were you before you came in here?

BRIGID: Outside. In the rain.

NIALL: And before that?

BRIGID: On the road, walking...

NIALL: And before:

BRIGID: In the water.

NIALL: —You went swimming out in this?

BRIGID: —I was asleep—I was *dreaming* of swimming—

NIALL: Oh, well that's an entirely different matter
altogether...

BRIGID: —And I woke up just now and it was dark—

NIALL: —Late night last night was it?

BRIGID: I was here.

NIALL: ...No you weren't.

BRIGID: Yes, I was.

NIALL: ...

BRIGID: —It was crowded—

NIALL: I remember faces...I would've remembered
your face in particular.

BRIGID: ...Can I open my (*"eyes now"*)?

NIALL: Not yet no:

BRIGID: …I sat in the corner, had too much to drink.
—I got sick in the bathroom and walked home in the
rain—

NIALL: —Home?

BRIGID: *Mirage*, where I'm staying. Know it?

NIALL: Sure, Jean Coyle, friend of mine.

BRIGID: Sure she is, but it's not Jean Coyle runs *Mirage*.

NIALL: Maybe it's not *Mirage* you're staying.

BRIGID: —It is, and Billy Reilly runs *Mirage* now.

NIALL: I don't know no Billy Reilly…

BRIGID: Well he knows you.

(BRIGID *opens her eyes;* NIALL *lets her.*)

NIALL: …Does he now? (*He moves behind the bar.*) Well
they're not here.

BRIGID: Who?

NIALL: —Your keys, my girl, your keys!

BRIGID: —Are you sure? I mean—have you looked?

NIALL: Of course I haven't looked for your God
damned keys…

BRIGID: —Then how can you know for *sure?*

Maybe they're on the floor, or *underneath* something.
—There's so much crap in here—

NIALL: Hey!

BRIGID: —they could be anywhere. —All I mean is how
do you know if you won't even look?

Can I? look?

NIALL: Suit yourself…

(BRIGID *does.*)

NIALL: —But you leave everything as you found it, understand?

BRIGID: ...Jesus, do you dust?

NIALL: Can't: I'm allergic.

BRIGID: What about health code?

NIALL: Do I look like a man who cares about health code?

BRIGID: You don't get many customers in here, do you...?

NIALL: You tell me; you were here last night.

BRIGID: ...It's like a museum, or a mausoleum...

NIALL: I call it my Memory Palace: "Memory Palace in Decay." That's from a poem by Keith Waldrop. I don't suppose you're familiar with his work.

BRIGID: *(Still looking)* ...It can't be good for you...

NIALL: Of course poetry isn't good for you...

BRIGID: No, all this—what *is* this—?

NIALL: Careful—!

BRIGID: —asbestos?

NIALL: It's only dangerous if you—

(BRIGID does:)

NIALL: —touch it...

BRIGID: Sorry...

NIALL: It's all right: just try not to breathe.

(BRIGID lifts a mortar and pestle off a high shelf; offers it up to him:)

NIALL: I used to be a pharmacist.

BRIGID: ...I'll bet you were... *(She returns it.)*

(A plunger now:)

NIALL: Put that back, please—!

BRIGID: I'm not going to break it—

NIALL: —Put it back, I said—!

BRIGID: Why do you keep a plunger on your wall?

NIALL: It's my father's...

BRIGID: Was he a plumber...?

NIALL: No, he was full of shit.

BRIGID: Oh: ha ha.

NIALL: —Yes, ha ha—now put it back.

BRIGID: *(Doing so)* —What's this?

NIALL: What does it look like?

BRIGID: ...

NIALL: Open it.

BRIGID: *(She does.)* It's a compass...
...It's beautiful.

NIALL: —Now put that back as well.

(BRIGID *does.*)

BRIGID: There seems to be a real nautical theme here. Are you fond of the ocean?

NIALL: No, but living on an island: there it is.

(BRIGID's *at the bar, near him now; she sits.*)

NIALL: —Give up?

BRIGID: ...Are we playing a game?

NIALL: Your keys—

BRIGID: Oh, no... *(She smiles.)* Not yet...

NIALL: I'll have to keep an eye out for you, then: lost things have a habit of turning up here.
...Drink?

BRIGID: I don't, thanks—drink.

NIALL: And last night was what, shore leave?

BRIGID: *(Flirting, perhaps)* A special occasion—a celebration...

NIALL: Oh, ah...

BRIGID: It was, yes... *(She smiles again.)*

NIALL: —Celebration of what, may I ask?

BRIGID: My freedom; my—liberation, you could say. Can I have a glass of water, please?

NIALL: Of course you may, my girl...

(NIALL pours it for BRIGID from the tap; brings it to her.)

NIALL: One hundred percent Key West tap water: nearly eighty percent water.
Lead is a *very* underrated mineral, I'll have you know...

BRIGID: Thank you, sir. *(Takes a sip:)* Delish.

(NIALL sits or leans near BRIGID.)

(A long and awkward moment—for her.)

NIALL: ...And now I suppose you expect me to talk to you.

BRIGID: What is it we've just been doing?

NIALL: Chit-chat, repartee. —I was right in the middle of a very good game of solitaire, I'll have you know—

BRIGID: By all means don't let me stop you playing with yourself.

NIALL: —You have a wonderful way of talking.

BRIGID: ...

NIALL: You realize that...?

BRIGID: Do I?

NIALL: Do you talk that way to everyone? or just to people you don't know? —Have we met before?

BRIGID: That's an old line.

NIALL: I'm an old man...

BRIGID: Not *that* old...

NIALL: —Where're you from?

BRIGID: Oh, here and there...

NIALL: Are you serious...?
Well there's no here *here*, my girl. —Just misquoting my good friend Gertrude Stein. She's a writer, you know.

BRIGID: Oh.

NIALL: *(Making fun)* Ah.

BRIGID: *(Making fun of his making fun)* Ah...

NIALL: Yes, she is.

BRIGID: —Does she come in here often?

NIALL: Not as often as you might think: she's dead.

BRIGID: ...Oh...I'm sorry.

NIALL: Don't be. She wasn't. Ms Stein was what you might call an unrepentant lesbian. What do you make of unrepentant lesbians?

BRIGID: I don't. Make much of them. —Listen, nothing against your friend Miss Stern—

NIALL: "Stein."

BRIGID: —right; but I need to find my keys and get the hell out of Dodge, so if you don't mind—

NIALL: Why?

BRIGID: ...?

NIALL: Why leave so soon? sit down—don't you like it here in Paradise?

BRIGID: —I don't. No. As a matter of fact, I hate it here.

NIALL: You "hate" it here?

BRIGID: —I *loathe* it here!

NIALL: Please don't spare my feelings—

BRIGID: *(Overlapping)* This has been the most miserable week of my entire fucking life!

NIALL: …And why is that, do you think?

BRIGID: You know…? I honestly do not know…
I have my theories, though.

NIALL: Tell me:

BRIGID: It's stupid, really—

NIALL: I would consider it a rare opportunity for, I don't know—

BRIGID: Mustaches.

NIALL: I beg your pardon?

BRIGID: There are too many men with mustaches here. It's like the '70s.

NIALL: —That's the reason you "loathe" Key West: mustaches?

BRIGID: The other day I was out walking, in the rain, and this guy—*with a mustache*—drives by in a pickup truck and flicks a cigarette at me.
Lit.
It's not a high-class environment, let's just put it that way…
…I sound like a snob.

NIALL: You do, but—

BRIGID: Sorry—

NIALL: —takes all kinds.

BRIGID: *(She smiles at this)* …

NIALL: …You know what I think:

BRIGID: What:

NIALL: You're bored.

BRIGID: No I'm not—

NIALL: Stands to reason: beautiful young woman without a young man—

BRIGID: —How do you know I don't have a young man?

NIALL: Do you?

BRIGID: …

NIALL: Or young woman, is it?—this is Key West, after all…

BRIGID: I don't think I know you well enough—

NIALL: —How long've you been down here so?

BRIGID: Three days. I told you: —long as it's been raining… Rain doesn't bother me, though; I prefer rain to sun any day.

NIALL: You do.

BRIGID: ("Yes.")

NIALL: Let me understand something: you've come to Key West and you don't like the sun?

BRIGID: Rain either, truth be told. —I don't like "weather," as a rule, as a topic of conversation. —I prefer rooms.

NIALL: (Snaps fingers) New York.

BRIGID: …?

NIALL: That's where you're from: New York City—am I right?

BRIGID: (Laughing) —Is it that obvious?

NIALL: It's your ("face")—

BRIGID: Oh, God—!

NIALL: A person gets to have a kind of a face on account of where she lives; and your face says "New York City."
Sorry. (*Studies her longer:*) —The Bronx.

BRIGID: (*Laughs*) —Well fuck you too!

NIALL: (*Laughing, too*) The Bronx was once quite beautiful, my girl—! Dutch farmland, the Iroquois nation...!

BRIGID: And you're wrong: I'm from New Haven.

NIALL: Oh my, it's worse than I thought...

BRIGID: But I grew up in New York; so that's very astute of you, very—perceptive...

NIALL: ...

BRIGID: In the Bronx.

NIALL: —You don't say!

BRIGID: —I do—I do say!

NIALL: You're not just telling me what you think I want to hear, now are you?

BRIGID: I don't know; I don't know you—what is it you want to hear...?

NIALL: ...Where in the Bronx did you say?

BRIGID: Are you familiar with the Bronx?

NIALL: I grew up in "the Brahnx."

BRIGID: —You don't say!

NIALL: I do *so* say!

BRIGID: Zerega.

NIALL: —Zerega. I know Zerega. I used to run through Zerega every morning in my football helmet on my way to school because this gang of Italians used to chase me and beat me just for being Irish.

Are you Italian so?

BRIGID: No.

NIALL: You look Italian—a little: the hair…

BRIGID: I thought you said I looked New York.

NIALL: The two aren't mutually exclusive, my dear.

BRIGID: Well I'm not. —I'm a *little* Italian. My mother's mother was Italian, I *think*, but I'm Irish all the way.

NIALL: …Ah.

BRIGID: …Oh.

NIALL: …Yes, well… You don't sound very "Oirish."

BRIGID: Well that's because I'm not. —I'm American.

NIALL: But you're also Irish…

BRIGID: Irish-American. You know what I mean.

NIALL: As long as we've got all the hyphens in place… (*He looks at her closely, deeply, for too long.*) …You'd have to be Black-Irish, that's what you'd have to be; with your hair…

BRIGID: (*Turns away*) …

NIALL: …Irish-American, you don't say.

BRIGID: —Eighty percent Irish. American; yes.

NIALL: That's a curious figure, "eighty"—how do you figure that figure?

BRIGID: Three out of four grandparents were Irish. And one of them was very fat.

NIALL: That's not very nice, you know…

BRIGID: "But seriously folks, I'll be here all week"…

NIALL: You were setting me up for that one? Were you setting me up?

BRIGID: No—

NIALL: *(A flash of anger)* —Don't you dare set me up, girl.

BRIGID: … *(She pulls away from the bar.)*

NIALL: …Because you're dealing with a world-class bullshitter here; and you can't bullshit a bullshitter… *(He smiles:)*

Did you never hear that one before?

BRIGID: …Can I have some more water please?

NIALL: You've not finished with that one yet…

*(*BRIGID *drinks the rest of her water down.)*

*(*NIALL *takes her empty glass.)*

NIALL: *(Whilst filling it)* …What do you do up there in sunny New Haven?

BRIGID: I attend Divinity School.

*(*NIALL *brings it to* BRIGID, *sets it down.)*

NIALL: *(Sits or leans)* I'm sorry: I thought you just said "Divinity School."

BRIGID: I did.

NIALL: Well.

BRIGID: Yes.

NIALL: You don't say…

BRIGID: Well, I did actually. —Twice—"say."

NIALL: —"Divinity School" …What are you studying to be, better than the rest of us?

BRIGID: A priest.

NIALL: "Priestess"?

BRIGID: Priest is fine.

NIALL: Or "priestperson," would you prefer? I know how you young women are these days...

BRIGID: Priest is fine, thanks.

NIALL: And what religion would it be that allows a pretty young girl like you to become a dirty old priest?

BRIGID: The Episcopal Church.

NIALL: *(Strikes bar)* —I might have known.

BRIGID: —What have you got against Episcopals?

NIALL: Oh now look: I've got nothing against the chosen frozen—they've a right to exist. Alls I'm saying is it rubs me the wrong way to see an 80% Black-Irish-American-Girl turning her back on the Holy Mother Church of Rome—

BRIGID: The Catholic Church won't ordain female priests; they condemn abortion, birth control; —they *insist* upon the virgin birth—

NIALL: —You don't believe in the virgin birth?

BRIGID: Not literally, no—

NIALL: —You believe in what, the gist of it?

BRIGID: I believe in the *metaphor* of the virgin birth.

NIALL: I believe that makes you an atheist, my girl.

BRIGID: *(Excitedly, sits forward)* The virgin birth is just a metaphor by way of the Greeks: Leda and the Swan, Persephone and the Serpent—they all have what are essentially virgin births. The most famous Gospel—of the four sanctioned Gospels—that mentions a virgin birth is Luke, written by a Greek for a Greek audience. There are virgin births all over the ancient world, but you don't see people killing abortion doctors in the name of Zeus.

NIALL: Not anymore, anyway.

BRIGID: Not anymore… You're very funny. —Or at
least you *think* you are…
Are you a believer?

NIALL: *(Backs off)* …

BRIGID: —I don't mean to freak you out—

NIALL: *(Overlapping)* No—

BRIGID: I'm curious, that's all—.

NIALL: …

BRIGID: Are you okay?

NIALL: *(Overlapping)* I know what you mean about the
Catholics…

BRIGID: What do I mean about the Catholics…?

NIALL: I was raised Catholic, and they committed all
sorts of atrocities on me.
It was the nuns, primarily…

BRIGID: It would have to be.

NIALL: I was born left-handed, you see, and every
day at school they'd tie the thing behind my back and
make me write with my right: "Write with your right!"
they'd shriek—the crows, the banshees…
I used to think, Is it because "right" is the same as *right*,
you know, as in a moral correctness? And if that's the
case and being left-handed is a sin like, then how come
"left" is not a homonym for evil?
Well it is, in Latin: *sinister* is Latin for "left"…
—The point is: all this fuss about left-handedness
because at the End of Days, God sets the goats to his
left, and the sheep to his right; and it's the goats he
casts down into hellfire eternal…
I spent my entire childhood feeling like a goat…
Some metaphor in a two-thousand year-old book and
I've got Satan's hand at the end of my arm.

BRIGID: …You see? the trouble literal-mindedness gets you into…?

NIALL: I've another if you have a minute:

BRIGID: Well—

NIALL: Sitting in class, daydreaming, twelve like, hunched over one of those inexplicable adolescent erections. It was a burgeoning bright tumescent spring day, and who should come strolling down the aisle but Sister Mary Frigidquim, slapping her twelve-inch ruler like a baton… She glances down at the conspicuous if I do say so myself bulge in my trousers—and she *presses* it—with her ruler! The bitch depresses the part of my pants that appears to harbor an erection—! Like it were nothing—! Like she were testing the firmness of a cake…

Now; an older man might've seen it for what it was. But I was a boy, and I near died of shame that day… All the blood rushed to my face—and away from a certain part of my anatomy thank you God. She looked at me, not even the slightest bit embarrassed, and she said: "You keep your eyes in the book, you."
—Can you imagine? "In the book"!
…I was reading Paul's First Letter to the Corinthians, if you can believe it: "He who marries does well. He who *refrains* does better"…
Are you celibate yourself so?

BRIGID: …

NIALL: You don't mind me asking—?

BRIGID: —No; I'm not. Are you?

NIALL: What? —Celibate? Go on!
I thought about becoming a priest, though…

BRIGID: Even after what happened with the erection?

NIALL: Even after!—you could say *because* of what
happened with that erection—and it was the celibacy
thing that kept me free…
I mean, why do that to yourself?

BRIGID: —I don't know—

NIALL: It's lunacy—

BRIGID: It's contrary to human nature—

NIALL: It's self-hatred is what it is—

BRIGID: It's a Papal ruling based on medieval West-
European economics.

NIALL: …Is it now?

BRIGID: There's no call for it whatsoever in the Gospels.

NIALL: Isn't there though?

BRIGID: None whatsoever.

NIALL: Well now…! How about that! The *cheek* of them
sneaky old Popes!

BRIGID: Mind if I smoke? *(Rummages in pockets for
cigarettes, lighter)* —The point is: any positive reference
to sex in the gospels has been excised…

NIALL: And why is that, do you think?

BRIGID: It's complicated, really…

NIALL: It would have to be.

BRIGID: It's the body-soul dichotomy: people who hate
the body are perceived as holier than those who love it.
I should know: I'm anorexic—or I used to be, anyway.
The body is the vessel that carries the soul on its
journey through the world. No more the real person
than the map of a country is the actual country. The
body is not the soul. The body most often *obscures*
the soul. —Since the dawn of time people have been

trying to strip away the body—through abstinence, mortification—to get at *who we really are*…

Burn the map, the thinking goes, find the country. *(She lights her cigarette.)*

NIALL: You really are a divinity student, aren't you?

BRIGID: You think I'm what, a nerd?

NIALL: —A what?

BRIGID: I don't know— "nerd"?

NIALL: —Ha!

BRIGID: I don't have my degree yet…

NIALL: Well you should have that. You should have that by now, I think…

BRIGID: *(She smokes)* …

NIALL: …I do disagree with you on one point, however: I think, if you get rid of the concrete, the flesh and the blood, that which you can see and touch and feel: what's left? Nothing but water and smoke…

BRIGID: …

NIALL: …God, I *know* I know you.

BRIGID: …

NIALL: The way you argue with me; the way you smoke that cigarette…

BRIGID: —I'm a lesbian, by the way.

NIALL: …

BRIGID: …

NIALL: …You don't say.

BRIGID: I did. Actually. Say. —You realize you say "you don't say" quite a lot?

NIALL: Well that's because you keep saying things that surprise me. —Why do you keep on doing that?

BRIGID: *(Shrugs and smokes)* ...

NIALL: ...May I ask you a question so?

BRIGID: Shoot:

NIALL: Did you walk through that door a lesbian, or was it something I said?

BRIGID: *(Laughs)* —Don't be cute!

NIALL: It's an honest question—

BRIGID: —Can I have another glass *("of water")* ?

NIALL: *(Taking glass)* ...Of course you may, my girl... Are you a recovering alcoholic, then? in addition to being an anorexic lesbian. —Sorry, it's just the way you take your water...

BRIGID: I'm not a lesb—I *am* a lesbian; I'm not an alcoholic. Now you've got me all mixed up...

NIALL: *(Laughing softly, filling water)* ...

BRIGID: ...You ask a lot of questions for a man whose bar is closed...

NIALL: ...How else do you get to know people, I think?

BRIGID: Do you know a lot of people...?

NIALL: ...?

BRIGID: You seem kind of—hermetic.

NIALL: ...That's only because I don't like people very much...

BRIGID: You've been very kind to me.

NIALL: That's because I don't *know* you yet... *(He brings her the water.)* Do I.

BRIGID: —Bridge.

(BRIGID offers NIALL her hand.)

NIALL: Sorry?

BRIGID: That's my name: it's short for Brigid.

(NIALL *takes* BRIGID'*s hand.*)

NIALL: I'm pleased to meet you—I can't call you
"Bridge," it's far too pedestrian...

BRIGID: Oh, ha ha—

NIALL: I could call you Biddy or Bridie; or the Latinate
"Brigitta"—and in Irish, the hard G: Brigg-id. *(Still
holding her hand:)*
...Or maybe I should call you *Saint* Brigid. —Would
you like that? "Saint Brigid," Patron Saint of Poets;
among other things... *(With his free hand he pulls a chain
out from under his shirt—it's around his neck. On it hang a
cross, and a key.)* Recognize this?

BRIGID: No. It's a key.

NIALL: Not the key, the cross. —*Your* cross: "Saint
Brigid's cross" it's called. She was a very famous saint.

BRIGID: I thought you said you weren't religious.

NIALL: I'm not; I'm Catholic.
—She was a pagan goddess first. —See? The cross is
like a compass: north south east and west, and in the
center: head of a pin... *(He smiles. He puts the chain
away.)* ...Brigid... And you may call me Niall.

(BRIGID *pulls her hand back:* NIALL *lets her:)*

BRIGID: Pleased to meet you, Niall...
And—

NIALL: Yes?

BRIGID: I think I will have that drink now.

NIALL: —You're going to make me break a sweat,
girl—

BRIGID: Sorry—

NIALL: *(As he goes)* —walking to and fro for water and drink—wine, then? wine? a finger or two of the filthy Chardonnay?

BRIGID: —Whiskey please, Mr O'Neill: my throat's a little sore from the—

NIALL: Oh, you poor girl—

BRIGID: —all that singing last night and—

NIALL: One hot toddy coming up—with lemon?

BRIGID: Yes please, thank you, Niall…

NIALL: *(As he fixes her drink)* …May I ask you another question so, Brigid?

BRIGID: …?

NIALL: How is it you've come to know my last name?

BRIGID: …Do I?

NIALL: You said it just a moment ago.

BRIGID: I must've read the sign.

NIALL: Which sign?

BRIGID: The sign outside.

NIALL: Oh no, dear: that sign says "The Second Coming."

BRIGID: Does it?

NIALL: It used to light up.

BRIGID: …

NIALL: —Who told you my name, Brigid?

BRIGID: I must've heard it somewhere. —Billy—

NIALL: "Billy Reilly"—

BRIGID: I was looking for a place last night, a quiet place to drink, and Billy Reilly mentioned your bar: Looks like a house from the road but inside you'll find a pub, he said. He must've said your name,

"Niall O'Neill," and it stuck with me because it's so—
redundant.

NIALL: …

BRIGID: …

NIALL: *(He smiles)* …It *is* redundant… That's precisely
what it is… *(He brings her whiskey to her:)* …In Irish, you
see, "Neill" is the possessive of "Niall," so when you
say "Niall O'Neill" what you're really saying is "Niall
of the family of Niall"…It's mad; incestuous, really,
like a whale eating its own tail…
As a child, the children were ruthless: you know, *Nile
O Nile O Nile O Nile,* round and round neverending—.
I used to think I'd been named after the Nile River in
Egypt, and despite all the teasing I felt quite proud…
And then I learned how to spell. And someone told me
"Niall" was just Irish for "cloud," and I went out of the
river and into the sky…

BRIGID: …What does my name mean in Irish?

NIALL: I don't know, exactly… We'll have to find that
one out, now won't we…

(A flash of lightning)

BRIGID: —Jesus!

NIALL: Calm down—

BRIGID: It's close—!

(Thunder)

NIALL: *(Shutting the windows)* Lightning won't come in
through the window, my dear—

BRIGID: —How do you know?

NIALL: We're in a flood zone—we ought to be scared of
drowning…

*(A long pause; the rain and wind is heavy; BRIGID calms a
bit.)*

(NIALL *watches* BRIGID.)

BRIGID: ...I'm sorry. I have this *fear*...

NIALL: ...It's far away now, over Cuba. It always rains harder over Cuba. And do you know why? Because they're Communists, that's why...

(Another flash of lightning, thunder.)

NIALL: You're safe here with me, my girl...

(BRIGID *and* NIALL *sit together, quietly.*)

(More of the storm)

(Then, he kneels:)

NIALL: *(Crossing himself)* "North, South, East, West." — Repeat after me:

BRIGID: *(Hesitates)* I'm Episcopal—

NIALL: Shut up—you might learn something:

(BRIGID *kneels too.*)

NIALL: "Jesus of Nazareth, King of the Jews,"

BRIGID: "Jesus of Nazareth, King of the Jews,"

NIALL: "from a sudden and unprovided for death"

BRIGID: "from a sudden and unprovided for death"

NIALL: "deliver us, O Lord."

BRIGID: *(Overlapping)* "deliver us, O Lord."

NIALL: Amen.

BRIGID: *(Almost together)* Amen.

NIALL: *(Sitting up)* ...There. Feel better?

*(More lightning, thunder. —*BRIGID *reacts, but calmer now.)*

BRIGID: ...When I was a girl, I wouldn't go to the bathroom during thunderstorms...

NIALL: ...Would you not?

BRIGID: I thought: if lightning can strike the reservoir, and the reservoir is connected through the pipes all the way to my house, and to my toilet... And the water in the toilet is connected to my body, well, when I—when I "pee"...then all it takes is one bolt of lightning in the Catskills and *pphhhhttt*, I'm toast.

NIALL: This was a very real fear of yours?

BRIGID: Yes.

NIALL: —And did someone ever give you the impression that electrocution via the Catskills whilst peeing was even a *remote* possibility?

BRIGID: I don't think so...

NIALL: You just thought—

BRIGID: *(Laughing)* It could happen!

NIALL: *(Laughing too)* It *could* happen—!

BRIGID: —Yes; why not?

NIALL: Why *not* you?—you could be the exception to the what, to the rule?

BRIGID: Lightning strikes—

NIALL: Aye, sometimes twice...

BRIGID: ...You think I'm what, weird?

NIALL: I would never call another human being "weird" ...Much less an anorexic lesbian priest afeared of pissing in storms.

BRIGID: That's not very funny.

(NIALL *chuckles softly.*)

BRIGID: —And I'm not anorexic anymore.

NIALL: Now you're just splitting hairs—

BRIGID: —And I've heard a few stories about you, "Niall O'Neill"...

NIALL: *(Quietly)* From who?

BRIGID: My father.

NIALL: Who's your father?

BRIGID: Your brother.

NIALL: …

BRIGID: …

NIALL: …How old are you?

BRIGID: It was a long time ago when I saw you last…I was a girl. I was playing on the floor by the door, in the morning, and you came into the apartment while the rest of the family was asleep. You had a key…
You had a long, black beard—you were a "hippie"; I thought you were God. You bent down with that long, black beard and you handed me a children's picture Bible…
"Don't tell your parents I was here."
And then you turned around and left.
I thought I'd dreamt it, except I had that Bible now.

NIALL: …I don't remember that—

BRIGID: It happened—

NIALL: —I'm not saying it didn't—

BRIGID: It happened, I'm *telling* you—

NIALL: It might have happened, I'm just saying—!
I don't—.
You're going to have to give me a minute on this one, Brigid…
…I don't remember a lot of things, much less things that happened twenty, twenty-five years ago—.
I'm not—. I'm *surprised*, that's all…
Look: I don't know what your father told you, but for a long time I was what you might call clinically depressed. In fact, I was mildly schizophrenic, in the

opinion of several doctors. I had black-outs where I did all sorts of God knows what and woke up in strange places. I hallucinated, had *extreme* paranoia—

BRIGID: My father said you were a pathological liar.

NIALL: ...Did he now...

BRIGID: He said you were in the witness protection program—

NIALL: Ah right: Harold would say that...

BRIGID: He said you killed someone—something involving drugs—do you deal drugs?—or I don't know, smuggle?

NIALL: ...

BRIGID: My mother used to say you were hiding from the Black Panthers...

NIALL: Oh, well, that's *very* exotic...

BRIGID: You were dating Huey Newton's girlfriend and the Panthers wanted you dead, so you stole your mother's collection of early-American coins and her Buick Century and headed out west. —Or *Key* West. —Or Mexico; or Alaska—nobody ever really knew for certain where you were...

NIALL: ...

BRIGID: Harold's dead, by the way.

NIALL: ...All right.
How?

BRIGID: Cancer. A year ago.

NIALL: He's only two years older than me—.

BRIGID: ...

NIALL: ...Why didn't—?

BRIGID: —We tried. We didn't know where you were—

NIALL: You could've hired someone—

BRIGID: We did: no one could find you: no bank accounts, no credit cards, no tax returns—you don't exist, Niall.

NIALL: How did you find me, then?

BRIGID: —Aren't you upset? —I just told you that your brother's dead—

NIALL: Of course I'm upset—

BRIGID: Did you two have a falling out? over what?

NIALL: Nothing—

BRIGID: Then why did you leave like that? why did you sneak into the house? why did you talk to *me* and give me that Bible...?

NIALL: Look, I'm sorry to disappoint you, Brigid, but there's no secret here: I was dating a black girl. Joyce wasn't Huey Newton's girlfriend, but she was black, which was bad enough for the Bronx Irish—and she's the one who stole your grandmother's car.

BRIGID: —And the coins?

NIALL: Forty bucks at a pawnshop, got me as far west as Chicago...

BRIGID: Did you kill anyone?

NIALL: At that point no.

BRIGID: How do you think a story like that gets started?

NIALL: Your father was the pathological liar. It's true: he lied all the time. Our mother lied—they all lied, the whole fucking clan did, it was what they did for conversation. They never thought they were lying, which is why they were so good at it—which is what the Irish do: they're too frightened, or maybe just too *sinister*, to *know* people. —You know? actually get to *know* them…? So they make up all sorts of charming lies to cover up their appalling lack of knowledge—.

BRIGID: Do you ever lie?

NIALL: You look so much like her—the hair…

BRIGID: …

NIALL: She was not a great fan of mine, your mother. —Does she know you're down here now?

BRIGID: No.

NIALL: Do you talk to her?

BRIGID: —Not if I can help it.

NIALL: …

BRIGID: …

NIALL: Well. *(He starts to clean up.)* It was nice meeting you, Bridge.

BRIGID: You want me to leave?

NIALL: I've got an early day tomorrow—

BRIGID: Doing what?

NIALL: —and I don't have much time for nostalgia. —Is there anything in particular I can help you with, Brigid?

BRIGID: My keys—

NIALL: We're closed.

BRIGID: I know that, but I left them here so—

NIALL: No—you're not listening: the bar's been closed over a year now; I don't run it anymore—I'm retired… This is where I live…
You couldn't have been here last night.

BRIGID: …

NIALL: So tell me the truth now: what do you want from me?

BRIGID: I stole a car.

NIALL: ...All right.

BRIGID: From my mother. Like you.

NIALL: ...Well.

...That's not stealing—that's adolescence. —Though in your case I'd have to say it's a somewhat protracted adolescence...

BRIGID: She doesn't know I stole it. —She knows it's gone, but she doesn't know it was me...

NIALL: —Why'd you steal it?

BRIGID: *(Shrugs)* We had a fight.

NIALL: About what, dear.

BRIGID: Doesn't matter.

NIALL: So stealing the car was an act of vengeance? — Are you a vengeful girl?

BRIGID: *(She looks for a cigarette)* ...

NIALL: Dump it then. Leave it. I know some people who'll take it, give you some cash; —go back to Divinity School and *you know nothing.* You had a breakdown of some kind, and you left New Haven for a little R & R—and you're feeling "much better now." ...No one will suspect you, an Episcopal priestperson.

BRIGID: I don't know if I can do that: I'm a terrible liar.

NIALL: I'll bet you are...

BRIGID: I don't think I could live with myself is what I mean.

NIALL: You can forget almost anything if you just put your mind to it, my girl.

BRIGID: ...

(After a moment, NIALL pours himself a drink, drinks it.)

(He has another.)

*(*BRIGID *watches him, a bit enviously…)*

(…So he pours a drink for her.)

(His hands shake as he brings it to her.)

(She notices.)

NIALL: It's a medication—. It makes my hands shake.

*(*BRIGID *takes the drink and drinks it.)*

BRIGID: …What kind of car do you drive?

NIALL: *(Laughs)* I'm not letting you anywhere near my car—!

BRIGID: I don't want to drive it—I don't want to steal it—

NIALL: It's a Jaguar.

BRIGID: A what…?

NIALL: That's the kind of car I drive: a black jaguar.

BRIGID: I know: I just didn't understand the word you used—

NIALL: —"Jaguar."

BRIGID: —You mean, "Jaguar".

NIALL: That's what I said: Jaguar.

BRIGID: Expensive car, the Jag-you-are…

NIALL: Not the one I've got: I got mine on the cheap.

BRIGID: …How?

NIALL: You know those police auctions where they sell off the cars they've confiscated? This is one of them: The Black Jag-u-ar…

BRIGID: Why'd they confiscate it?

NIALL: —The fuck does it matter why they confiscated it?

BRIGID: It matters a lot. —I mean, aren't you curious?—
who owned it before you, why the police had it?

NIALL: I know who owned it before me—and I'm
saying *it doesn't matter.*

BRIGID: —To *you.*

NIALL: To me.

BRIGID: So tell me: it matters to me:

NIALL: (*"No."*)

BRIGID: —Why not?

NIALL: You'd be—

BRIGID: What?

NIALL: I don't know— "disturbed".

(BRIGID *claps her hands expectantly.*)

(NIALL *smiles:*)

NIALL: …They didn't so much confiscate as—retrieve
it…
From the water. —Gulf side, pitched off Route 1,
heading south through the Keys…
And a man was in it.

BRIGID: Jesus…

NIALL: Yes; well…

BRIGID: Was it an accident?

NIALL: Not unless he'd been accidentally shot in the
back of the head.
Twice.

BRIGID: God…

NIALL: I cleaned it up—the seats were soaked all to
hell. But other than that she's a steal.

BRIGID: Where is she?— "it"?

NIALL: Round the back, under a tarp. —I don't drive her.

BRIGID: …Why not?

NIALL: She's haunted.

BRIGID: …Come on—

NIALL: It's very real to me!

BRIGID: …

NIALL: Sometimes, when I used to drive it, there'd be this kind of—movement, you know?—in the mirror, over my shoulder—a *blur*…

BRIGID: …

NIALL: I take it you don't believe in ghosts.

BRIGID: Not really, no.

NIALL: —You believe in souls but not in ghosts?

BRIGID: I believe in ghosts in the *metaphorical* sense—

NIALL: If it's a metaphor, my girl, then it's not a ghost!—you're trying to have it both ways—!

BRIGID: I think you can only be haunted by what you know; by what you've done. So unless you were the one who killed that man in his car, you've got nothing to worry about.

NIALL: …

BRIGID: …

NIALL: That would be quite a story, now wouldn't it…?

BRIGID: …

NIALL: —Mind-reading:

BRIGID: What?

NIALL: Does it happen—yes or no—

BRIGID: No.

NIALL: Stigmata?

BRIGID: Not a chance—

NIALL: —Spontaneous combustion—

BRIGID: No fucking way—

NIALL: —I think it's beautiful: flesh—poor, mudmade flesh—*bursting* into flames... Doesn't it, I don't know, just—wake you right up?

BRIGID: Has it occurred to you—?

NIALL: What:

BRIGID: —that spontaneous combustion is a scientific impossibility considering the fact that our bodies are nearly eighty percent water?

NIALL: Oh well, you can make statistics say just about anything...
Telepathy? telekinesis?

BRIGID: I think people are more perceptive than they realize—

NIALL: —This is *exactly* what's wrong with your generation! You never take a stand on anything! —Say what you will about the '60s—

BRIGID: Was I saying anything about the '60s—?

NIALL: At least we believed in things. We had faith, passion. We got our hands dirty—

BRIGID: And look where that got you.

NIALL: ...

BRIGID: ...I said "you" but I meant your generation...

NIALL: ...

BRIGID: ...

NIALL: You think I'm what, crazy?

BRIGID: No—

NIALL: Because I have been institutionalized… More than once…

BRIGID: …

NIALL: —But so was Sylvia Plath, and she was a right-on woman; not to mention our friend James Joyce…

BRIGID: Was he institutionalized?

NIALL: No, but his daughter was.

BRIGID: …

NIALL: —Alls I'm saying is there are more things in heaven and earth—and there's proof.

BRIGID: Where?

NIALL: The people themselves.

BRIGID: —But you're forgetting that people lie.

NIALL: …

BRIGID: For instance, I'm not in Divinity School. I made that up.
Too.

NIALL: …*Why*, Brigid…?

BRIGID: I was scared.

NIALL: …

BRIGID: I say things when I'm nervous; I exaggerate—.

NIALL: …

BRIGID: They're not lies; they're—embellishments.
I want to be a priest, one day. —Like what you
said about my family—*our* family: we can't help it.
Whatever's happened, we always think of something
better.

NIALL: Better than what…?

BRIGID: Once, when I was a girl—around the side of
my house I turned this corner into bright sunlight and

I felt my head explode, or melt away. Like someone
had pulled the plug in a tub and all the water rushed
out and all the inside of me just rushed out... My brain
was like the leaves on a tree, my spine its trunk, my
bones its branches—the whole world was made of *me*;
and I was nothing—a cloud, water...
I was not "aware" but—it was *within my grasp* to
understand that God was in me. God was *not* me, but
somewhere inside all this mess of blood and bone
and confusion was a trace of Him, left over from the
garden—a clue...
Isn't that what we're all looking for? a clue?
...I slept for days after that... The doctors said I had a
seizure.

NIALL: It sounds like you did have a seizure...

BRIGID: I have seizures all the time: I'm epileptic.

NIALL: ...Are you now?

BRIGID: *("Yes.")*

NIALL: —Alcohol brings them on, you know.

BRIGID: I know; that and strobe lights, thanks. —And
nicotine. *(She lights a cigarette.)* I'm medicated, Niall—I
wouldn't dream of imposing on you like that...

NIALL: What sort of medication?

BRIGID: Are you familiar with medication for epilepsy?

NIALL: —Now listen: two minutes ago you were an
Episcopal priest—

BRIGID: I want to be a priest; I told you that.

NIALL: So you're not in school—?

BRIGID: I'm in college—I *was* in college—

NIALL: —And you didn't steal your mother's car?

BRIGID: Oh no, I did do that—

NIALL: Well thank God something's true—

BRIGID: —And then I crashed it. I totaled it. —I left
it, on the side of the road, in some water, actually; a
lake…
I hitchhiked down here.
I got here three days ago—and I've been on the beach
ever since…

NIALL: …You don't look like someone who's been in a
car wreck.

BRIGID: I'm a miracle, I guess. *(She smiles.)*

NIALL: —Do you have some I D?

BRIGID: …?

NIALL: Anything with a picture on it—a name? a
driver's license?

BRIGID: —As it turns out, no, I do not have a driver's—

NIALL: A student I D then? —Library card?

BRIGID: —I lost everything—in the car—

NIALL: You don't have anything to prove who you are?

BRIGID: —I don't exist, Niall! —You should know
what that's like. —And while we're on the subject of
paranoia: didn't you have an accent?

NIALL: …

BRIGID: When I came in here before you had a thick
what-do-you-call-it— "brogue."

NIALL: This is my voice is my voice my dear—

BRIGID: Now you're just putting it on—

NIALL: —I am putting no such thing on!

BRIGID: Two minutes ago you sounded just like some
guy from the Bronx!

NIALL: I am some guy from the Bronx!

BRIGID: So what's with the phony brogue?

NIALL: —I am Irish from the Bronx!

BRIGID: *(Calming, somewhat)* …I'm angry…
I lose my temper…
My mother loses her temper and that's what I *fucking*
hate about her—!

NIALL: …

BRIGID: Do I look like her? You said before that I look
like her—

NIALL: Not so much look like her as act like her—

BRIGID: Did you two ever have something together?

NIALL: …

BRIGID: I'm sorry—

NIALL: I'd like you to go.
…I'm not mad at you, I'm—

BRIGID: —Did you love her?

NIALL: …

BRIGID: You loved her and she loved you—am I your
daughter?

NIALL: *(Exploding)* —You've got quite the nerve—!

Coming into my house—!

BRIGID: It's all right—!

NIALL: Coming into *my* house and digging—!

BRIGID: —I said it's all right…! *(She's standing near the
door.)* …I've got my answer…

NIALL: …How old are you?

BRIGID: Twenty-three.

NIALL: You could be—.
You could be…I honestly do not know for certain…

BRIGID: ...I'll leave—

NIALL: No—

BRIGID: I shouldn't have come—

NIALL: —Sit down—

BRIGID: I have to go—

NIALL: Where are you going? where could you *possibly* have to go now?

(BRIGID *begins to cry.*)

(NIALL *moves to her.*)

BRIGID: ...

NIALL: ...You really are a miracle, aren't you...?

(NIALL *reaches out and touches* BRIGID, *gently, on the head.*)

BRIGID: ...

NIALL: Do you need money...?

BRIGID: I don't want any money—

NIALL: Don't be embarrassed to ask me—

BRIGID: *(Overlapping)* —"your father."

NIALL: ...

BRIGID: ...Do you have money?

NIALL: How much do you need?

BRIGID: Depending on what you've got...

NIALL: Five hundred? a thousand?—just say it:

BRIGID: Okay.

NIALL: Okay.

(NIALL *removes the chain—with the key and the cross— from around his neck, and disappears through a dark upstage door.*)

(BRIGID *waits, alone.*)

(He returns—the chain is around his neck again; he's counting out some bills.)

NIALL: Here:

BRIGID: Thanks. —I'll pay you back.

NIALL: It's a gift.

BRIGID: No—I'll pay you back:
I promise.

Two:
"South"

NIALL: Hello?

BRIGID: Hello?

NIALL: Hello—Brigid?

BRIGID: —Hi!

NIALL: What are you doing out here…?

(BRIGID and NIALL approach each other in the dark, along the beach, in a mist.)

BRIGID: —Niall?

NIALL: How are you…?

BRIGID: I'm fine. —My light broke.
How are you?

NIALL: I'm fine, too…

BRIGID: That's funny…

NIALL: What is?

BRIGID: Nothing; just the way we're—I don't know, "talking."

NIALL: Are you looking for me?

BRIGID: I went for a walk, as soon as the rain let up, with a flashlight which as you can see has just—

(BRIGID's *light flickers.*)

NIALL: Bridge—

BRIGID: —busted. —If you shake it—like that—it—

NIALL: Brigid—

BRIGID: —flickers—see? it flickers. —My mood, Niall, it's so *improved!*

NIALL: …

BRIGID: Why are you staring at me like that?

NIALL: …I see you've got yourself a slicker.

BRIGID: A—? yes.

NIALL: And the lightning?

BRIGID: What about it?

NIALL: Doesn't frighten you anymore?

BRIGID: —Not this kind of lightning: no it doesn't.

NIALL: What kind of lightning would you call this?

BRIGID: It's the kind that jumps around up there like—

NIALL: Watch your step.

BRIGID: (*She doesn't*) —I don't know, like "neural activity."

NIALL: …We're talking about the weather here?

BRIGID: I'm glad it's stopped raining…

NIALL: It'll start again…

BRIGID: …No one's every accused you of being an optimist, have they?

NIALL: …Would you like to sit down?

(*A stone, or a fallen tree trunk.* BRIGID *hesitates.*)

(NIALL *sits first, wipes the seat with the seat of his pants, moves over.*)

(*She sits beside him.*)

BRIGID: —Do you think that, as a culture, the Irish have an unnatural obsession with the weather?

NIALL: *(He thinks about this)* Yes.

BRIGID: That's it: "yes"?

NIALL: Yes. *(He stares at her a long time.)*

(BRIGID turns away.)

BRIGID: ...My—father used to talk about the weather. Some days that'd be all he'd talk about. When he was sick, we were caring for him at home, I was supposed to visit after exams and my mother put him on the phone: his voice—he sounded like an old woman...
"I understand you've got rain where you are..."
Can you imagine?
...We talked about the weather, for a minute, and then hung up. And then he died like two days later...

NIALL: ...Rain, when it's hot, is not such a bad thing...

BRIGID: ...No; you might even say that rain is good...

NIALL: ...

BRIGID: ...Well I don't care what you say: I think the storm's over...

NIALL: ...Do you know it's a major symptom of schizophrenia to divine too personal a meaning in the weather?

BRIGID: —Were you schizophrenic...? The other night you said you'd been institutionalized—

NIALL: —That was a long time ago...

BRIGID: And what was it, a mistake?

NIALL: Everyone's entitled to an opinion...

BRIGID: So you consider mental health a matter of opinion?

NIALL: —I like to think instead I was ecstatic—
"ecstasy," in the religious sense; I felt transcendent,
transfigured, and not a bit sick...

At the time I remember wishing I were a religious man
so that I could explain it that way. But I didn't have the
words... How could I say, as a modern man, agnostic
if not atheist, "Look here everyone, I'm hearing voices
and they're telling me grave things about the world
and my place in it and I swear it's all coming from
God"...

...They gave me electroshock treatment; I got better...

BRIGID: ...

NIALL: ...Do you have something to tell me, Brigid?

BRIGID: ...What do you mean?

NIALL: Where've you been these last two days...?

BRIGID: I don't know—

NIALL: You don't know where you've been—?

BRIGID: I know, but—

NIALL: I thought I would've seen you again by now—

BRIGID: You're seeing me now.

NIALL: I know. All the same; I thought you might've
dropped by...

BRIGID: ...

NIALL: —I woke up the next morning and thought I'd
dreamt it—I thought I'd seen a ghost. —Why would I
think that?

BRIGID: ...

NIALL: Where've you been? —Do you remember?

BRIGID: Of course I remember—what kind of question
is that?

NIALL: —Where, then?

BRIGID: Where would I go? I walked around the island—

NIALL: Where?

BRIGID: Here and there, saw the sites—

NIALL: Which sites?

BRIGID: Houses, you know—homes—

NIALL: Whose homes?

BRIGID: Famous homes, literary homes—homes of dead people. —You think I'm, what—?

NIALL: No—

BRIGID: —lying? —I bought a fucking slicker, Dad!

NIALL: —That's not fair—!

BRIGID: How is it not fair?

NIALL: —That money was a gift—!

BRIGID: A pay off's more like it—

NIALL: Do you know how many children I've got?

BRIGID: ...No
...This is fascinating; please:

NIALL: You're not special... That's all I'm saying...

BRIGID: ...I used the money to get a room, and a bed to sleep in... The rest I have on me—I can show you if you'd like. (*She doesn't.*)

NIALL: I was worried about you...

BRIGID: ...

NIALL: —You're in trouble; anyone can see that—

BRIGID: What kind of trouble could I be in?

NIALL: I don't know—

BRIGID: *(Overlapping)* —I'm not pregnant. —And it would have to be an immaculate conception of some kind considering—

NIALL: I said I don't care to know—

BRIGID: *(Overlapping)* —I haven't had sex with anyone—*ever*—!

NIALL: …

BRIGID: …I went walking, the last two days… Around the island.

I'd no idea the maps were so wrong. Not wrong: but, blind. They left out the important streets—the lanes and alleyways and dirt paths…I took these paths and came out someplace new: a street I'd seen but now I saw it differently. One road took me to an old house where an old man with a tank and an oxygen mask stood leaning up against a ladder, breathing hard… He looked at me and then he closed his eyes…

The whole time it was raining…

The island's like a maze, but when I got lost I didn't feel so lost at all. I love it here.

NIALL: Do you…?

BRIGID: *("Yes.")*

NIALL: That's quite a change from the other day…

BRIGID: I know; I've changed my mind—.

NIALL: …

BRIGID: …

NIALL: …Shall I tell you a story?

BRIGID: I don't know. —I guess.

NIALL: …The Irish believed in a place called Hy-Brazil. An island. Some call it Tir Na Nog, but that always sounds like a flavored coffee to me. —All that matters is that it was an island off the west coast of Ireland—an

island off an island, so already we're dealing in myth...
And Ireland in those days of flat-earth theory was the
edge of the world, at least to the West Europeans; so an
island past Ireland—west of west—this was truly an
impossible geography...
There was a poet named Oisín. He was the son of
a warrior named Finn. Oisín would travel with his
father, and fight, and chronicle their fighting in song.
One day they were out riding and they saw this
beautiful young woman approaching, riding her white
horse across the waves—naked, of course. Up out of
the ocean, out of the west she rode. They stopped to
admire her riding technique... It was obvious at a
glance she was a goddess. She rode up on the dry land
and looked down at each man from atop her steed. She
came to Oisín, and—recognized something. "Come
with me," she said.
He didn't have to think twice.
He said good-bye to his father, his friends. They were
sad to see him go, but they knew they would've done
the same. —This was a goddess, for fuck's sake! So
Oisín climbed behind her on this white horse, coiled
his hands round her front, and off they rode together
across the waves, into the west, to Hy-Brazil...
Now in Hy-Brazil, Oisín lived in a perfect state of bliss.
He never aged a day, and never suffered hunger, nor
sickness, nor sorrow of any kind. Yet, little by little,
he began to miss his family, his home. He went to
the goddess one day—her name was Niamh—and
he told her of his pain. She felt pity for her lover,
and she granted he could take her horse to Ireland
for just a quick holiday. —"But never get off that
horse!" she warned. "For if you do, if you so much
as touch the tip of the toe of your foot to the ground,
all the years you've cheated death will fall upon your

back—at once." And she snapped her fingers like a thunderclap…

He promised he would remain always on that horse, and away he rode over the waves to Ireland…

What he found there shocked him: in his absence, a thousand years had passed. While he had stayed young, his father and his friends, countless generations of Irish, had all died. A new Ireland had sprung up, full of churches and bishops and God avenge us the English. Oisín cried aloud in anger and despair for all that had changed and been lost, and in his grief he fell, toppled down from his horse.

And when his body hit the ground it was just as the goddess had said: he aged a thousand years; he turned to dust, blew away in the wind…

BRIGID: …

NIALL: …Do you see what I'm saying?

BRIGID: *(Standing)* …You don't want me here—

NIALL: Bridge—

BRIGID: It's okay; you don't need to tell me a story— you can say what you're thinking—

NIALL: This has nothing to do with you, it's my—

BRIGID: *(Overlapping)* "It's my fault"—it's not like we're dating—!

NIALL: I need you—

BRIGID: What—?

NIALL: —I need you to lower your voice—*please!*

BRIGID: My voice?—who's going to hear me—? There's nobody out here, Niall—it's just you and me— *hello!*

NIALL: —*Quiet!*

(NIALL *grabs* BRIGID's *arm.*)

BRIGID: Let *("go")*! *(Frees herself)* —You're not my
father! You may have fucked my mother twenty years
ago but my real father raised me and now he's dead!
So don't worry, I don't want to stay with you. I don't
want to live here—you freak!—*murderer!* —What
did you think I was going to do? hit you up for child
support? move in? Open up a flower shop in your God
damned kitchen?

NIALL: *(Quietly)* —I'm warning you:

BRIGID: —What are you going to do to me? what could
you *possibly* do to me now…?

(NIALL transforms: all bluster and anger gone.)

(He turns away from BRIGID.)

NIALL: …Do you know why it's called "Key West"?

BRIGID: I don't want to play any more word-games,
Niall; I don't want to hear any more stories from you…

NIALL: *(Overlapping)* It's from the Spanish, "Cayo
Hueso": Island of Bones—

BRIGID: —It's because of the white coral wash on the
beach—it's a fucking metaphor—!

NIALL: —I called your mother last night.

BRIGID: *(She sits again, reeling)* …

NIALL: …On the phone, last night, and—

BRIGID: That must have come as quite a shock to her—
Stir up any old, you know, longings?

NIALL: Bridge—

BRIGID: —Any sparks fly?

NIALL: She said you were dead.

BRIGID: …

NIALL: *(He looks at her)* …She said you were dead, and
then she hung up. I never even said who I was—.

BRIGID: Well, she's lying—

NIALL: Why would she lie, Brigid? Why would she tell a stranger that you're dead if you are not?

BRIGID: —Because she wishes I was dead—! Because this was just the *latest* thing—the latest disappointment—and that's when she said I was like you—that I'd end up just like you—

NIALL: She didn't say you were "dead to her"; she said you died, in a car crash, in South Carolina. Last week. They found your car in a lake; in the water…

BRIGID: …

NIALL: …You have to go now—all right?

BRIGID: I'm Brigid, Niall. I'm your daughter—

NIALL: *(Shaking head)* Brigid's dead—. You're dead—

BRIGID: —I'm not—I'm *obviously* not dead—!

NIALL: —How is that obvious? —How is *any* of this obvious?

—You could be a ghost!

BRIGID: What?

NIALL: You're the spirit of my daughter—haunting me because of what I've done to you—!

BRIGID: …I'm not a ghost, Niall. —Touch me:

NIALL: …?

BRIGID: Go on: touch me—I'm real—

NIALL: —They touched the wounds of the risen Christ—! *(He stands tall in the sand and meets her gaze: a lunatic, or a prophet.)* —They touched the wounds of the risen Christ and the flesh was no less real!

BRIGID: …

NIALL: ...You have to go now...I'll buy you a ticket, I don't care—

BRIGID: Niall...

NIALL: —What, are you laughing?—are you crying?

BRIGID: ...You're right...

NIALL: What am I right about...?

BRIGID: I give up. This is too hard...

NIALL: It certainly is...

BRIGID: —It's ridiculous!

NIALL: It is. —Tell me:

BRIGID: I'm sorry—okay? None of this was supposed to—. I don't know how it got this far...

NIALL: How far? what got far?

BRIGID: My mother's right: I'm Brigid; I'm your daughter, and I died like five days ago.

NIALL: ...

BRIGID: I'm dead.
I'm a ghost. (*She laughs.*)
I told you it's ridiculous...
—I don't expect you to understand; that's why I haven't *said* anything till now—.

NIALL: ...

BRIGID: —Think: how did I find you in the first place?

NIALL: How...?

BRIGID: ...I was driving, in the rain. South, as far as I could go... Over a bridge—I fell asleep—.
Then I'm in the water. I can't open the doors. Water's flooding in through the dashboard, through cracks in the doors—I can't open the doors—I'm punching the glass with my fists—screaming—the water's rising at

my neck and the car is sinking...I'm *screaming* and then
my mouth is full of water...
Next thing I know I'm on the road.
I'm standing. —I'm wet. —*I'm fine.*
I walk for hours in the rain and night, and there's not
a soul out walking. Cars pass me by every once in a
while. Thumb's out—no one stops. No one *sees*...
I keep walking...and I'm not hungry or hurt or tired.
And I realize: I'm not alive anymore. That's how it
hits me—like when you fish a word off the tip of your
tongue, you know: "I'm dead," and I hardly noticed...
...And because I'm heading south I kept walking
and somehow I got here, and I saw you through the
window and I—opened the door...
I asked for my keys because I couldn't think of an
honest way to tell you the truth...

NIALL: ...

(NIALL *kneels in front of* BRIGID *in the sand.*)

BRIGID: What are you doing, Niall...? Get up.

NIALL: ...

(NIALL *takes* BRIGID's *hand.*)

(*A moment; he looks up.*)

NIALL: It's starting to rain again.

Three:
"East"

NIALL: Let me get the (*"lights"*) —

BRIGID: —Wow.

(*Books everywhere. The walls are books.*)

NIALL: Yeah.

BRIGID: Books...!

NIALL: I know...

BRIGID: What is this? I mean—

NIALL: It's my padded cell.

BRIGID: —Sorry?

NIALL: My studio.

BRIGID: Oh, it's—

NIALL: It certainly is...

BRIGID: "Books"—!

NIALL: It's cluttered is what it is—

BRIGID: —It's *intimate*. —Do you sleep back here?

NIALL: No.

BRIGID: —What's the bed for then?

NIALL: Hm?

BRIGID: The bed:

NIALL: Oh: inspiration.

BRIGID: Ah. Ha ha.

NIALL: Yes. It's just a room. —It's an old house—the walls are made of shipwreck wood—the island used to live off shipwrecks—

BRIGID: Niall.

NIALL: I'm sorry, I just—
I don't—.

BRIGID: —Do you mind if I *("sit")* ?

NIALL: No; please: —let me just *("clear away some space")*—

BRIGID: —What do you do here? in your studio? —I mean, other than read.

NIALL: I write.

BRIGID: What?

NIALL: I *write.*

BRIGID: —Really?

NIALL: Yeah.

BRIGID: What do you write?

NIALL: Poems.

BRIGID: You write poetry?

NIALL: I write poems.
Would you—?

BRIGID: —God, yes!

NIALL: I was offering to read you a poem.

BRIGID: Oh; I thought you were offering me a drink.

NIALL: —I could. I could get you a drink. Would you like—? —Do you drink?

BRIGID: Oh. —Yes: I drink.

NIALL: Oh, right. Of course you do. —The usual?

BRIGID: Yes. Please.

NIALL: Right back— *(He exits.)*

BRIGID: *(Calling after)* —Know what, Niall? I think I'll just have water…!

NIALL: *(Pops his head in)* Sure?

BRIGID: Yeah.

NIALL: …Are you all right so?

BRIGID: I'm fine.

NIALL: Right back. *(He's gone again.)*

(The bar is adjacent to the room, so we can just make out NIALL *in shadow, getting her a glass of water.)*

(BRIGID, of course, can't see him. She's having a closer look at the strange things in this room…)

(He pours himself a shot or two of something; drinks it.)

BRIGID: *(Calling off)* —What about you?

NIALL: *(Off)* —What?

BRIGID: Are you all right?

NIALL: I'm a bit light-headed…!

BRIGID: So am I…

NIALL: —What?

BRIGID: I said I'm sorry to hear that!

NIALL: It's just not every day—! You know—?

BRIGID: —I should hope not!

*(*NIALL *returns with a glass of water.)*

NIALL: *(Spilling some)* Shit—

BRIGID: It's all right—

NIALL: —I'm sorry, my hands—

BRIGID: Thanks. *(She takes the drink.)* What is it…?

NIALL: …?

BRIGID: You said medication the other night. Is it an anti-psychotic?

NIALL: It's epilepsy. Like you.

BRIGID: Epilepsy?

NIALL: —You think I'm psychotic?

BRIGID: Do you have seizures often?

NIALL: No… Not unless I'm excited. *(He smiles.)*

BRIGID: …Oh.

NIALL: *(Laughing)* —Ah!

BRIGID: Yes…

NIALL: Well, that—or drinking heavily.
That's a hundred percent Key West tap water, you know, nearly eighty percent water—

BRIGID: Stop it, Niall... Okay? I'm still Brigid...

(BRIGID's *touching* NIALL's *hand, to soothe him.*)

NIALL: —"Unassailable strength."

BRIGID: I'm sorry?

NIALL: That's your name, in Irish, the mudder tongue.
—I looked it up while you were gone the other night:
"Unassailable strength," Brigid...
...Makes me think of a ship at sea.

BRIGID: I don't feel very strong.

NIALL: —But you are!
You'd have to be—to be doing what you're doing,
what you've done...
Does it feel different?

BRIGID: Does what feel...?

NIALL: You know:

BRIGID: Oh...

NIALL: —Doesn't it?

BRIGID: No. Yes. —Not really.

NIALL: You know, I had no idea? before, when I was
talking to you—I had absolutely *no fucking clue!*

BRIGID: ...That I was your daughter?

NIALL: No—that you were dead! That you *are* dead! —I
suspected you were my daughter—I suspected that the
moment you came in—I *knew* without knowing it—.
But I *never* would've guessed you were a ghost; you
seemed so *("alive")*—

BRIGID: —How could you know?

NIALL: It makes sense, though...I mean, the clues;
looking back over the last few—

BRIGID: —You know what? it's all right: let's not talk
about this now, okay?

NIALL: ...Am I making you nervous?

BRIGID: —A little.

NIALL: All right...
I understand...

BRIGID: ...

NIALL: ...What should we talk about then?

BRIGID: —I like this room.

NIALL: *(Smiles)* Liar...

BRIGID: I do—it's *your* room—

NIALL: It's too many books, I know—

BRIGID: Why are there no windows in here?

NIALL: —There is one.

BRIGID: Where?

NIALL: Behind the bookcase there.

BRIGID: Which bookcase?

NIALL: That one there: philosophy. —No, psychology.
—All the "P"s, really.

BRIGID: Doesn't do much good there, now does it?

NIALL: It comforts me all the same. —You know, in
case of I don't know *fire*...
I find them a distraction.

BRIGID: Fires?

NIALL: No—

BRIGID: Books?

NIALL: —Windows.

BRIGID: Ah. Mmm.

NIALL: Yes. —Ha ha!

BRIGID: —A distraction from your poetry?

NIALL: —You really are the same, aren't you?

BRIGID: ...

NIALL: I mean, as you were before...
Are you an angel?

BRIGID: ...

NIALL: Don't be shy:

BRIGID: I'm not an angel, Niall...

NIALL: —Not yet!

BRIGID: —Not ever. —It's not like the movies: angels
aren't people.

NIALL: —They've no blood.

BRIGID: ...?

NIALL: I remember that from school: "Dee angels, dey
do be having wather in deir veins."
The nuns taught me that.

BRIGID: Right. Well look, I'm not an angel: okay? I'm
Brigid.
—Let's take this slower...

NIALL: ...

BRIGID: Can I hear a poem?

NIALL: —Of mine?

BRIGID: *("Yes.")*

NIALL: Ah no don't think so...

BRIGID: You just offered—

NIALL: I know! but you see I've changed my mind.

BRIGID: —Does it embarrass you? —I don't mean to—

NIALL: We'll do it later, okay?

BRIGID: ...What do you write about, then? Is that all
right to ask?

NIALL: Oh this and that, here and there...

BRIGID: ...This is something you don't like to talk about...

NIALL: ...Personal things; I write about—symbols, from everyday life.
You wouldn't find it interesting...

BRIGID: I would...

NIALL: ...

BRIGID: We can talk about something else, if you'd like—

NIALL: —It's just that I've never had anyone back here before, that's all...

BRIGID: ...No one?

NIALL: *("No.")*

BRIGID: I find that hard to believe...

NIALL: It's true.

BRIGID: ...No lovers? —No friends?

NIALL: Not in a very long time...

BRIGID: ...Well thank you. I'm honored.

NIALL: —No *I'm* honored—*I'm* the one who should be honored here tonight! *(Laughs)*
Really, I had no *idea* you were dead...!

BRIGID: I'd no idea you were a poet!

NIALL: —You don't say!

BRIGID: I *do*, I *do* say! —It makes perfect sense, though: your attention to—your faith in words.

NIALL: ...Okay.

BRIGID: What:

NIALL: I'll give you a poem now.

(NIALL *goes to a desk drawer, pulls out a messy cardboard folder. He flips through loose pages, selects one for a reason. He hands it to* BRIGID.)

NIALL: Read it in your head.

(BRIGID *takes it from* NIALL, *reads it slowly.*)

(*He's nervous, moves about the room; he won't look at her, won't sit down.*)

(*When she's finished reading she hands it back to him.*)

BRIGID: (*Quietly*) It's beautiful.

NIALL: …You don't like it.

BRIGID: I do.
I'm just not sure I understand it, that's all—

NIALL: What's to understand? it's a poem—. (*He puts it back in the folder, replaces folder in the drawer, shuts the drawer hard.*)

BRIGID: I'm sorry, Niall.

NIALL: —Did it scare you? is that why…?

BRIGID: …A little.

NIALL: …It's supposed to scare you. (*He smiles:*) A little.

BRIGID: What does it mean?—explain it to me: all that imagery—

NIALL: (*Overlapping*) —Why do you have to keep asking me so many questions?

BRIGID: …?

NIALL: If you don't mind me asking: if you're dead— if one is dead—I should think one should just *know* certain things. About poems, and people—

BRIGID: I'm not omniscient, if that's what you mean.

NIALL: You're not.

BRIGID: No.

NIALL: Not even the *slightest* bit?

BRIGID: No.

NIALL: That's too bad…
Can you perform miracles?

BRIGID: No.

NIALL: Have you tried?

BRIGID: *("No.")*

NIALL: —You have got to be kidding me!

BRIGID: —I'm not a saint, Niall!

NIALL: —Miracles would be the first thing I'd try! *(He pushes her glass of water closer to her.)* Red or white.

BRIGID: I'm not Jesus Christ, Niall…

NIALL: *(Smiles; takes water back)* …I know you're not…

BRIGID: …

NIALL: Can you fly? can you travel great distances in time and space?—is time and space just a metaphor for you—?

BRIGID: I don't think so—

NIALL: How do you travel so?

BRIGID: I walk. All ghosts walk. That's why we never get very far from where we've died.

NIALL: —But *you* did. You got far. South Carolina is very far away by foot.

BRIGID: I suppose.

NIALL: —How did you do it, then?

BRIGID: I had someone special to visit… Someone very important who was very far away…

NIALL: —You had a *mission*.

BRIGID: You could say that—

NIALL: But you're not through with your mission, now are you...

BRIGID: I don't know...

Why are you smiling at me so much?

NIALL: —Do you walk through walls?

BRIGID: No.

NIALL: Have you tried?

BRIGID: —No, and I'm not planning to any time soon!

NIALL: —Will you not try anything fun at all, *at all?*

BRIGID: —I can not walk through walls, Niall!

NIALL: —How do you know if you haven't bloody well tried!

BRIGID: *(Laughing)* All right.

NIALL: *(Laughing too)* Good!

(BRIGID *gets up, composes herself.)*

(*And walks into the wall—or more precisely, a bookcase.)*

BRIGID: Ow.

NIALL: Damn.

BRIGID: Shit.

NIALL: —Are you hurt?

BRIGID: —You see? *(Rubbing her nose)* Now I've gone and hurt myself for you...

NIALL: *(Rubbing her nose too)* Poor girl...

BRIGID: *(Laughing)* Poor nose...

NIALL: *(Laughing too)* Poor nose, poor soul—is there nothing special about you *at all?*

(BRIGID *and* NIALL *are too close; she pulls away.)*

BRIGID: ...I liked your poem, Niall. —Really...

NIALL: ...

BRIGID: —Do you publish?

NIALL: Sometimes.

BRIGID: Where? Maybe I've read something of yours—

NIALL: I doubt it…

BRIGID: You'd be surprised.

NIALL: I use a pseudonym.

BRIGID: Like what.

NIALL: I use more than one. —I don't want to get my ego involved.

BRIGID: …Is that what you do for a living, poetry?

NIALL: Yes: I'm a very wealthy poet.

BRIGID: So you don't make any money off of poetry?

NIALL: Not one bleeding cent.

BRIGID: What about drugs?

NIALL: —What about the fucking drugs!

BRIGID: —Do you have any?

NIALL: …

BRIGID: …Pot, or something? We could smoke it—you know, to relax.

NIALL: You want to?

BRIGID: Yeah…

NIALL: You want to smoke?

BRIGID: If you have any…

NIALL: I've got—I don't have marijuana; I've got ecstasy.

BRIGID: …

NIALL: You've done it, right? —Kids love ecstasy—the non-religious kind, the secular, synthetic little ecstatic pill—.

Would you like some?

BRIGID: *(Hesitation)* All right.

(NIALL moves to a small strong box, set in the bookcases perhaps, or under the bed.)

(He kneels to get at it.)

(He takes the chain with the cross and key from around his neck.)

(And he opens the strongbox with the key.)

(…Rummaging about now:)

NIALL: …I keep some for guests like…
—There she is…

(NIALL withdraws a cigar box from inside the strongbox.)

(Inside the cigar box: a ziplock bag with a few tablets.)

(He closes and locks the strongbox, returns the chain to his neck.)

(He hands BRIGID the bag.)

NIALL: Bottoms up.

(BRIGID opens the ziplock bag.)

NIALL: —Wait: let's grind it up first—it'll enter the bloodstream faster. —Do you want to do it that way?

BRIGID: Yeah.

NIALL: Okay. Right back.

(NIALL exits, back to the bar again.)

(He removes the mortar and pestle from the wall shelf.)

BRIGID: Can I dim the lights in here…?

(BRIGID does.)

(NIALL returns with the mortar and pestle.)

(He takes the bag from her, drops a few tablets in the pestle, begins to grind it down.)

NIALL: —You've done this before, right?

BRIGID: *("Yes.")*

*(*NIALL *lays the powder out now; rolls up a bill and hands it to* BRIGID.*)*

NIALL: Ladies first:

*(*BRIGID *does it, but with difficulty.)*

NIALL: —Are you all right?

BRIGID: *(Coughing)* —Yes—

NIALL: You sure?

*(*BRIGID *nods.)*

(She sits now at the edge of the bed.)

NIALL: Here: drink some.

*(*BRIGID *does.)*

NIALL: Maybe it's not fine enough... *(He snorts it.)* —oh, it's fine. *(Sits on the bed beside her.)* It won't be long... You'll see... Just wait... It'll feel like heat, at first...rhythmic, in your chest...rolling, like waves... like you're mad in love...like you see someone you love walking towards you down the street... It'll make you feel *better...*

BRIGID: ...

(A long pause here while BRIGID *and* NIALL *wait for the drug...)*

(...After a while:)

NIALL: ...This has turned into a really extraordinary evening, hasn't it?

BRIGID: ...It's almost morning.

NIALL: —No!

BRIGID: —It is—

NIALL: The room gets a lovely sunrise... You'll see. I'm not sure how it's managed, but somehow the light gets through...

(BRIGID *laughs.* NIALL *laughs with her.*)

NIALL: ...Whenever I heard voices in the past I never replied... That, I thought, would invite a world of trouble... In the Old Testament, God calls His chosen in the middle of the night and the brave ones answer: "Here I am"...

Here I am, Brigid...

Do you have something to tell me?

BRIGID: Like what?

NIALL: The truth?

BRIGID: ...I don't know...

NIALL: Yes you do...

BRIGID: ...

NIALL: All right, be coy.

—Do you feel it? Rolling, like waves...

BRIGID: ...Yes...

NIALL: How about I ask you a few yes-or-no-type questions so:

BRIGID: Fine:

NIALL: Was Jesus Christ a virgin birth?

BRIGID: Yes.

NIALL: —Really?

BRIGID: Yes.

NIALL: —You sure?

BRIGID: Positive: it was a miracle.

NIALL: So Christianity's the right religion? —I mean, you're not going to give me one of those "every religion has a grain of truth" explanations—

BRIGID: Every religion does have a grain of truth, but—

NIALL: Oh, Jesus Christ—! *(He covers his mouth.)*

BRIGID: It's all right.

NIALL: Is it...? You sure?

BRIGID: I told you, I'm not God.

NIALL: I know you're not...
So Christ was crucified? Christ rose again?

BRIGID: Yes. And yes.

NIALL: And will He come again?

BRIGID: Of course.

NIALL: Has He come again already? Is He here on Earth right now?

BRIGID: I don't know; what do you think?

NIALL: I think this information's bound to piss a lot of people off...

BRIGID: Well it sucks to be them...

(NIALL laughs.)

NIALL: ...You must've really been something, when you were alive...
Were you funny?

BRIGID: I don't know; I'm like I am now, I guess...

NIALL: I bet people loved you. —Were you popular?

BRIGID: "Popular"? in school?

NIALL: Did the boys like you?—or the girls?

BRIGID: I'm not a lesbian. —I said that when I thought you were—hitting on me.
I don't know what I am...

NIALL: …You're beautiful.

BRIGID: No I'm not—

NIALL: You are… That's the worst kind of sin—to be beautiful and think you're not…
…What did you want to be when you grew up?

BRIGID: Besides a priest? Nothing. I would've ended up like you, I guess.

NIALL: …

BRIGID: …I'm sorry.

NIALL: It must have been difficult, not knowing…

BRIGID: It was a comfort most of the time. No matter how bad things were, and they were bad most of the time, I always knew there was a *reason*. There had to be a reason
…I had that fantasy all kids have: that their parents aren't their parents—but I fixated on my father. I would imagine, going to bed at night, that you or someone like you—*my real father*—was out there. Somewhere. And if I could just hold on long enough, if I could wait and listen and look—for *clues*—maybe one day I'd find you…
Or you'd find me…
I thought a lot that I was crazy.
I used to wonder if you'd forgotten me. Because if you knew how bad I felt—you'd come and save me. Right? —But you never came—. *Why?* Didn't you care? And if you didn't care—if my own father didn't care about his daughter—what was I, then?
So I went looking for you—everything I did wrong, and I did a lot of things wrong, was my way of trying to find you. I thought—without thinking—if I just fucked up bad enough, you'd come and punish me. Right? Or we'd meet in a ditch somewhere, under a bridge or in jail, and you'd be just as screwed up as I

was. But it wouldn't matter because we'd be together, finally, and I could punish you... *(She's crying softly. After a moment.)* ...Did you love me at all?

NIALL: I can help you. *(He gets up, begins pacing the room.)* It's within my power to help you... I've never done it before...

BRIGID: ...?

NIALL: You're going to have trouble believing this. But I want you to keep an open mind and an open heart—. Do you promise you won't be frightened?

BRIGID: ...All right.

NIALL: ...All my life I knew I was destined for great things. I didn't know what. Or how. I didn't know what my calling would be. So I waited. I wanted to keep myself open—to callings. I wandered and looked and listened. People thought I was a "freak" or a "loser," but I knew I was just biding my time. One day—I was living here in Key West, I was thirty-three years-old—I'm out in my boat, waiting for someone, and I'm looking out over the waves, into the west, daydreaming... The sunlight bouncing on the waves like a heartbeat, like a brilliant conversation... And I fell in the water. I was having a seizure—and I drowned in the water.

I came-to in the coral reef at night. Who knows how much time had passed? All about me the beautiful things of the deep: dark fish and the black sand and the moon above me through the murk and weeds—and I realize: I'm breathing water. Like a fish, like a fetus— water in and out of my lungs, water for blood—.

I rise, against my will—I wanted to stay where I was— but I'm floating up to the boat, and I climb in, and I choke on air. I cough it all up, vomit up the sea—and in that instant I'm born again...

Now all this happened for a reason.

And it was not obvious to me at the time like you think it should be—in movies, or books. No voice out of the clouds said to me: "This is who you are." But—.
Gradually, as I went about my daily life, I began to recognize myself: driving in a car, sitting in a bar: Do you know who this is? sitting right beside you, madam?
It's Jesus Christ, madam. Pleased to make your acquaintance.

BRIGID: …

NIALL: …You're the first person I've ever told…
It feels wonderful to tell the truth, doesn't it?
I've been hiding it. Hiding from it, because of what it might mean. But now here you are. And you've come to me for a reason: to tell me it's true.

BRIGID: …

NIALL: But also for a reason I don't think even you understand:

(BRIGID *moves away from* NIALL.)

NIALL: —Hey, don't be frightened, okay? —Are you? it's okay…I'm not ("*going to hurt you*") —. I'm still Niall…
Don't you see how happy you've made me?
—I can help you!
I can give you back your life—I can *resurrect* you!
And when you're alive again you can take all the money in there—

(NIALL *give* BRIGID *the key and cross from around his neck; he puts it around her neck.*)

NIALL: —take it, it's yours—I don't need it anymore.
—Because you're my daughter, Bridge, and it's your due…!

And you can go away from here and start over
someplace new—and you'll *never* end up like me…
Okay?
Is it a deal?
—Come here: *(He raises his hands up, then lays his palms
upon her face.)* I do love you, Bridge…

(A moment)

(And then NIALL *begins to have a seizure.)*

*(*BRIGID *holds him for some time, on the bed, until his
seizure subsides.)*

(She lays him out. Waits)

(…)

(After a long time, she gets up.)

*(She seems to contemplate opening the strongbox with the
key around her neck.)*

(But she doesn't.)

*(Instead, she removes the key from the chain, places it
carefully on the bed beside him. She keeps the cross.)*

(She exits the room, then exits the bar.)

(…By now we should see that it's coming on dawn.)

(It's still raining.)

(As lights fade, he begins to wake up.)

END OF PLAY

www.ingramcontent.com/pod-product-compliance
Lightning Source LLC
Chambersburg PA
CBHW052213090426
42741CB00010B/2525